❧ A FRESH, FUN, FASHIONABLE SPIN ON ORIGAMI ❧

Girligami

CINDY NG

❖ A FRESH, FUN, FASHIONABLE SPIN ON ORIGAMI ❖

Girligami

CINDY NG

WATSON-GUPTILL PUBLICATIONS / NEW YORK

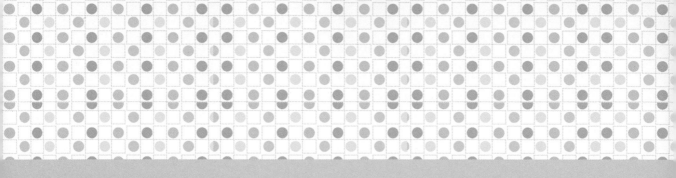

Senior Acquisitions Editor: Julie Mazur
Editor: Cathy Hennessy
Photographer: Simon Lee
Photo shoot art director: Chin-Yee Lai
Designer: Chin-Yee Lai
Production Manager: Alyn Evans

Published in the United States by Watson-Guptill Publications, an imprint of the Crown Publishing Group, a division of Random House, Inc., New York.
www.crownpublishing.com
www.watson-guptill.com

Library of Congress Cataloging-in-Publication Data

Ng, Cindy.
  Girligami : a fresh, fun, fashionable spin on origami / by Cindy Ng.
    p. cm.
  ISBN-13: 978-0-8230-9238-3 (alk. paper)
  ISBN-10: 0-8230-9238-0 (alk. paper)
  1. Origami. I. Title.
  TT870.N483 2009
  736'.982--dc22

                              2008022143

Watson-Guptill Publications books are available at special discounts when purchased in bulk for premiums and sales promotions, as well as for fund-raising or
    educational use. Special editions or book excerpts can be created to specification. For details, please contact the Special Sales Director at the address above.

Printed in China

First printing, 2008

1 2 3 4 5 6 7 8 / 15 14 13 12 11 10 09 08

Acknowledgments

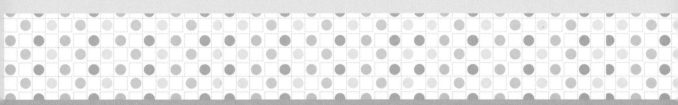

THANK YOU...

Regina Brooks, my agent, for believing in my potential.

Julie Mazur and Cathy Hennessy, my editors, for your creativity, guidance, and feedback.

Origami USA editor Marc Kirschenbaum for reviewing the instruction guides.

The entire Watson-Guptill team: sales, marketing, design, and production for your input and hard work.

Favorite Printing and PDQ Print Copy Mail for printing my origami samples and papers.

Mel Lim for being the best adviser and confidant.

$\mathcal{C}$ontents

Introduction:

MAKING THE CONNECTION

I have always thought of origami as a clever and beautiful art form. It has a rich history that dates back to the first or second century AD in China and gained prominence in the fifteenth century, when high-class Japanese samurai warriors practiced it as a form of gift-giving at banquets. However, I could never understand why origami continued to be such a popular pastime. I thought about it for a long time and came up with my own theory.

When I was ten, I really wanted to wear a pair of high heels because I thought I would look cool, but never found the occasion to get a pair (truth: my mother wouldn't let me). Now that I am old enough to wear heels, I still have to dream about looking cool in them—because the reality is, I can barely walk in them! There is one consolation, though. If I can't walk in them, I can at least fold them. This is why I started folding high heels. While folding shoes, I stumbled upon folding ice cream cones, which brought back fond memories of first dates, and excursions with girlfriends celebrating life's joys and sorrows (which of course then made me hungry for real ice cream). Each new project brought memories to mind, which in turn inspired other new projects.

Origami has always been an interesting way to engage and connect with our dreams, memories, and desires. As we fold origami creations, we think about what they represent, and the connections to our past and future lives. All with just a simple piece of paper.

Girligami has twenty all-new origami creations to make with easy to follow, illustrated step-by-step instructions. The projects are inspired by the world of delicious sweets, wacky critters, high-tech gadgets, falling in love, and the fashion runway. And have you ever wondered what to do with a cool piece of origami that you have just made? Well, now you can turn them into little gifts for yourself or your friends. This book has super fun and easy projects to make from your folded designs—there is everything from jewelry, to greeting cards, to hanging notepads. All the projects in the book are easy enough for curious beginners and intriguing enough for seasoned enthusiasts. This is the origami book I have always dreamed of having. So get ready: New and old memories are about to unfold at your fingertips.

Why I love origami

Origami is a vehicle of creativity and innovation for me. It creates beautiful and satisfying results in minutes, not to mention the fact that a piece of paper is quick and easy to find!

Here are some of the things origami can do for you, too:

Origami …

- fosters your visualization skills
- calms your nerves as you focus on folding (and not on whatever is stressing you out)
- tricks you into learning geometry
- increases your self-confidence as you master increasingly difficult models
- entertains you when you are procrastinating
- gives you thoughtful, pretty, economical gifts for family and friends

I hope you find origami as fun and engaging as I do. Happy folding!

Essential Tips

Here are some helpful hints to make your origami folding a great experience!

GET YOUR ORIGAMI PAPER!

Each model in this book uses original, one-of-a-kind origami paper, provided in the back of the book. But what do you do when you run out of paper? Well, I thought of that. Just go to www.girligami.com, enter the secret password (origirl), and print as many papers as you want. Print them on regular copy paper, or go high-end with better quality paper (for example, thin photo paper). You may want to practice on paper you print yourself first, and save the glossy paper in the book for after you have mastered the steps.

Note that some models, such as the In Hearts We Trust heart on page 71, and the Foxy Pumps on page 87, have both small and large versions. It is easier to start with the large version and then move to the small one after you've got it down.

BE CAREFUL!

Before you start folding, you'll need to trim your origami paper to size, so you should grab a pair of scissors. Or, if you want to be ultra precise, you'll need:

* craft knife (available in any crafts store)
* metal ruler
* cutting mat

Take your time, follow the outline, and cut carefully. It is important to start your model with exactly the right size paper. Always use the craft knife or scissors with caution. Children should be supervised or assisted by an adult.

BE CLEAN!

Origami paper likes a flat, clean surface. Work on an oil-free table or countertop, or even a hardcover book.

VISUAL LEARNING

Begin by orienting your paper exactly as shown in the first step. It is also recommended that the first time you try a model you use the same paper pattern as shown in the instruction (some models have a few different patterns to choose from).

USE THE DASHED LINES AND ARROWS

Dashed lines show where to fold, while arrows show in which direction to fold. When you see a circle with an arrow, the circle indicates where to pinch or hold the paper as you fold in the direction of the arrow.

FOLD IT, BABY!

First impressions are everything! Your origami paper's very first fold quickly commits to memory, so it helps to be precise and neat. Keep your origami in shape by running your thumbnail along each fold several times.

LOOK AHEAD

Review all the steps before you start folding a model. Then, as you're folding, it helps to keep looking ahead to the next illustration to see what should be created once you have completed the step you are working on.

BE PLAYFUL, PATIENT, AND PERSISTENT!

Don't take yourself too seriously—otherwise, if you do origami is zero ounces of fun. If you're feeling frustrated, take a break and come back to it later.

How to Use This Book

1. Flip through the models to find one you like.
2. Carefully tear out the appropriate origami paper in the back of the book (or go to www.girligami.com and print your own paper).
3. Trim your paper to size with scissors.
4. Follow the directions to fold, crease, squash, flip, and/or rotate.
5. Stand back and admire. Or, if you are feeling frustrated, take an ice cream or chocolate break and come back to it later.
6. Go to page 91 and turn your model into jewelry, cards, ornaments, and more.
7. Share your origami with someone you love, like, or have a crush on. Wink wink.

How Not to Use This Book

The sweets and treats on pages 17–27 may look delicious and yummy, but please do not eat them! In fact, no items in this book are edible. Keep the models well away from curious toddlers and babies.

How Hard Is It?

If you are new to origami, you may want to work your way through the book in order, as the earlier projects tend to be easier than the later ones. Each chapter also gets harder as it progresses. Origami is very individual, however; one person may find a project easy while someone else may find it challenging, and vice versa. Remember, if you get stuck on a project, you can always move on to another and come back to it later.

ACTION SYMBOLS

 dashed line: A dashed line indicates where you need to fold or crease.

―――― **solid line:** A solid line shows where a crease has been made that now serves as the guide to where the edge of your origami paper should align.

This symbol indicates that the paper needs to be flipped over. When the symbol is on the side of the origami paper, it means flip over from side to side, and when it is on the top, it means flip over from top to bottom.

 This symbol indicates that the origami paper needs to be rotated clockwise.

 This symbol indicates that the origami paper needs to be rotated counterclockwise.

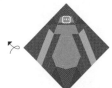

Flip Over from Side to Side

Flip Over from Top to Bottom

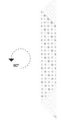

Rotate Clockwise

Rotate Counterlockwise

crease: To fold and unfold the paper, leaving a line or ridge to serve as a guide for a future fold.

fold: To bend your sheet of paper over, under, behind, or on top of itself so that one part covers another. This creates the framework for an origami model.

COMMON FOLDS

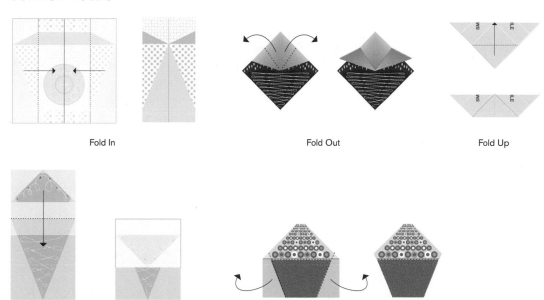

Fold In

Fold Out

Fold Up

Fold Down

Fold Behind

Collapse: For this fold, pinch sides of paper where indicated with circles and carefully bring them in and down to meet the bottom edge, as shown by the arrows. Look at the illustrations to see the collapse in progress.

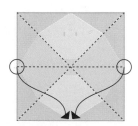

WHAT TO FOLD

Valentine Hearts

origami paper on page: 113
number of sheets needed: 1

Share a sweet message without the sugar. Send messages of love with this collection of candy hearts:
let it be, let's kiss, cool, whatever, all mine, smile.

1

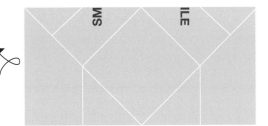

Flip over from side to side.

2

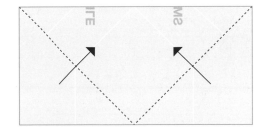

Fold the bottom corners up to the center.

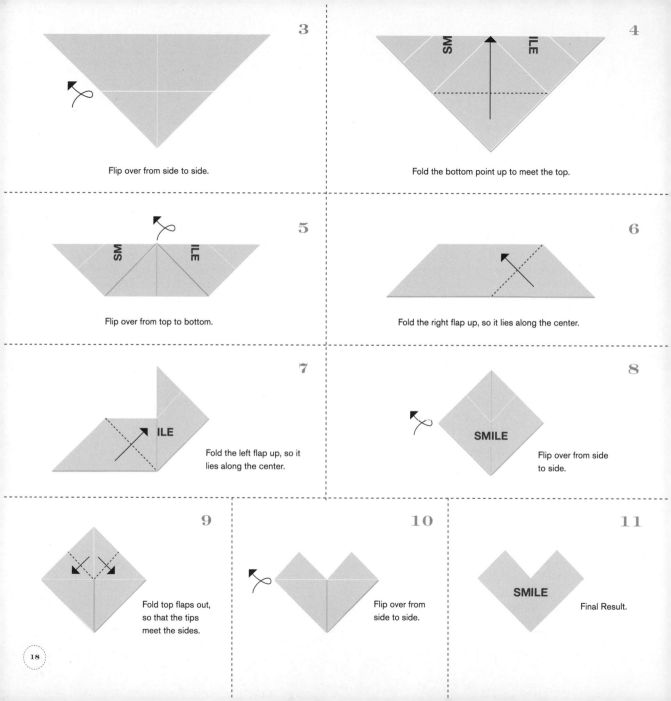

3

Flip over from side to side.

4

SM ILE

Fold the bottom point up to meet the top.

5

SM ILE

Flip over from top to bottom.

6

Fold the right flap up, so it lies along the center.

7

ILE

Fold the left flap up, so it lies along the center.

8

SMILE

Flip over from side to side.

9

Fold top flaps out, so that the tips meet the sides.

10

Flip over from side to side.

11

SMILE

Final Result.

NO VALENTINE? NO FEAR.

Here are five fun things to do next Valentine's Day, whether or not you have a valentine!

* Exercise: swim, walk, or run.
* Make a date with your best friend to visit a museum.
* Treat yourself to your favorite dessert.
* Give yourself a facial, manicure, and pedicure.
* Curl up with a great novel.

Sweet and Swirly Ice Cream

✳

origami paper on pages: 115 & 117
number of sheets needed: 1

I scream, you scream, we all scream for ice cream! There's no need to wait for a special occasion to eat ice cream. It's great for an afternoon out with friends, a first date, or just a sunny day.

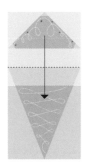

1

Fold the top down, using the pattern as a guide.

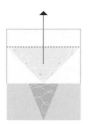

2

Fold part of the flap back up, using the pattern on the other side as a guide.

3

Fold the top corners behind, using the pattern as a guide.

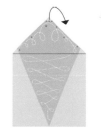

4

Fold the top tip behind, using the pattern as a guide.

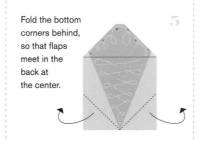

5

Fold the bottom corners behind, so that flaps meet in the back at the center.

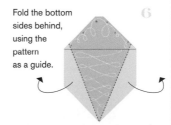

6

Fold the bottom sides behind, using the pattern as a guide.

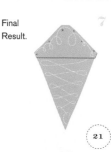

7

Final Result.

21

Cool Cupcake

*

origami paper on pages: 119 & 121

number of sheets needed: 1

Share your colorful cupcake with friends. After all, food tastes better when you share it!

1

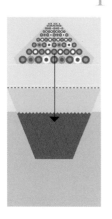

Fold the top down, using the pattern as a guide.

2

Fold part of the top flap back up, using the pattern as a guide.

3

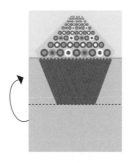

Fold bottom section behind, using the pattern as a guide.

4

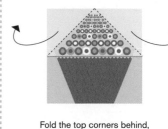

Fold the top corners behind, using the pattern as a guide.

5

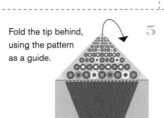

Fold the tip behind, using the pattern as a guide.

6

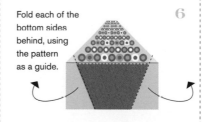

Fold each of the bottom sides behind, using the pattern as a guide.

7

Final Result.

Tasty Chocolate-Covered Strawberry

✳

origami paper on pages: 123 & 125
number of sheets needed: 1

These desserts are the best. Chocolate-covered strawberries are a delicious and healthy way to indulge. These origami versions are fun to make and have the added bonus of having zero fat and zero calories!

1

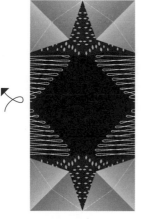

Flip over from side to side.

2

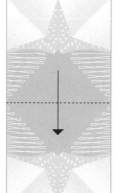

Fold in half. Unfold.

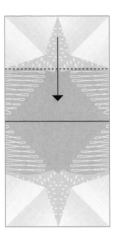

Fold top edge down to meet
newly formed crease. Unfold.

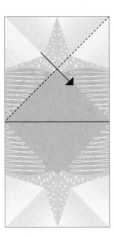

Fold top diagonally to meet
right edge. Unfold.

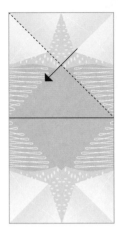

Fold top diagonally to meet
left edge. Unfold.

Pinch sides of paper where indicated with circles. Carefully push the two sides in while bringing the
top edge down, following the creases. Look at the illustrations to see the collapse in progress.

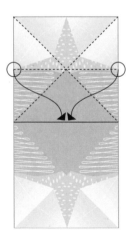

7   Repeat steps 3-6 for the bottom.

8

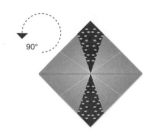

90°

Rotate model 90 degrees counterclockwise.

9

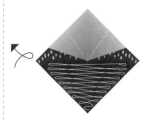

Swing bottom two flaps (top layer only) up to meet top.

10

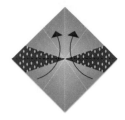

Flip over from side to side.

11

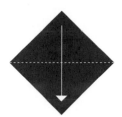

Fold top layer down to meet bottom.

12

Fold top flaps (top layer only) out, using the pattern as a guide.

13

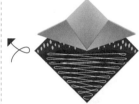

Flip over from side to side.

INDULGE FOR REAL

Fondue comes from the French word *fonder*, meaning "to melt." Craft your own chocolate fondue, and dip strawberries in for a tasty dessert.

Ingredients
* 1 cup heavy cream
* 12 ounces semi-sweet chocolate, chopped
* 1 teaspoon vanilla

Heat the cream in a fondue pot (or a medium saucepan) over medium-low heat until hot, about 2 to 3 minutes. Then add the chocolate and stir until it is melted and smooth. Stir in vanilla.

Serve with fresh strawberries, bananas, apple wedges, or pound cake. Serves 6 or more.

14

Fold top flaps out, using the pattern as a guide.

15

Final Result.

Bobo Panda

*

origami paper on page: 127
number of sheets needed: 2

My name is Bobo. I attend UCB (not University of California Berkeley, but University of California Bobo).
I spend my days growing bamboo to prevent global warming.

MAKE THE HEAD

1

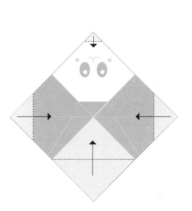

Flip over from side to side.

2

Fold the four corners in, using the pattern
on the other side of the paper as a guide.

3

Fold the bottom
edge up, using the
white line on the
other side
as a guide.

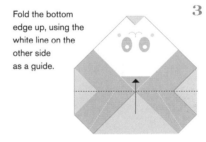

4

Fold the sides
up to meet in
the center.

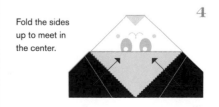

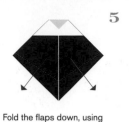

5

Fold the flaps down, using the white line on the other side as a guide.

6

Fold the bottom point up.

7

Flip over from top to bottom.

8

Final Result.

MAKE THE BODY

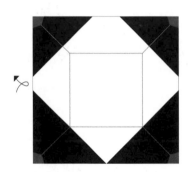

1

Lay the paper down as shown (make sure point of the white square is at the bottom). Flip over from side to side.

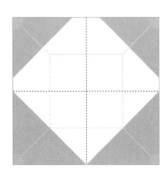

2

Fold in half horizontally. Unfold. Then fold in half vertically. Unfold.

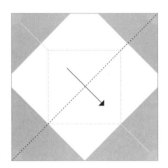

3

Fold top diagonally to meet right edge. Unfold.

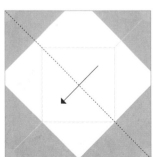

4

Fold top diagonally to meet left edge. Unfold.

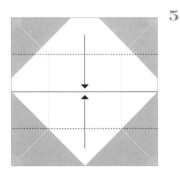

5

Fold the top and bottom edges to the center. Unfold.

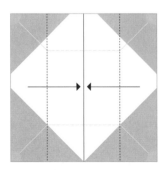

6

Fold the side edges to the center.

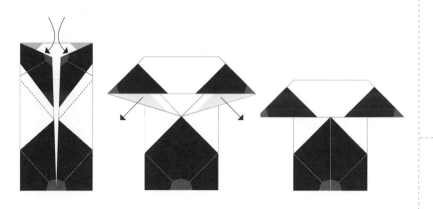

Open the top layer and insert your index fingers. Carefully spread the upper portion apart and fold down. Look at the illustrations to see the collapse in progress.

Repeat step 7 on the lower section.

Fold the side flaps up to meet in the center.

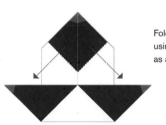

Fold the flaps out, using the pattern as a guide.

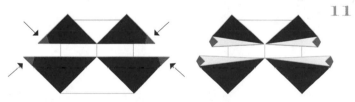

Spread apart the layers of the paws, and fold their tips in. Look at the next illustration to see this in progress.

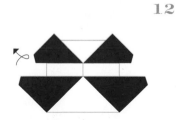

Flip over from side to side.

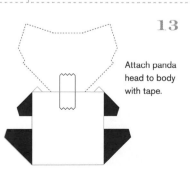

Attach panda head to body with tape.

Final Result.

Coca Koala

origami paper on page: 129
number of sheets needed: 2

My name is Coca. Everyone at school loves to call me Coca-Cola and, because I am a good sport, I offer my friends a cold beverage.

MAKE THE HEAD

1

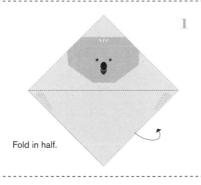

Fold in half.

2

Fold top behind, using the pattern as a guide.

3

Fold sides diagonally behind, using the pattern as a guide.

4

Fold the sides and the bottom point in, using the pattern as a guide.

5

Spread apart the layers of the ears, and tuck pointy ends in.

6

Final Result.

1

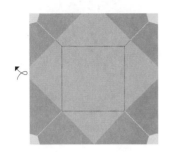

Lay paper down as shown (make sure point of inner gray square is at the bottom). Flip over from side to side.

2

Fold in half horizontally. Unfold. Then fold in half vertically. Unfold.

3

Fold top diagonally to meet right edge. Unfold.

4

Fold top diagonally to meet left edge. Unfold.

5

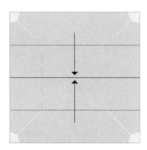

Fold the top and bottom edges to the center. Unfold.

6

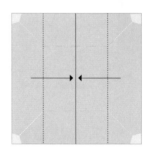

Fold the side edges to the center.

7

Open the top layer and insert your index fingers. Carefully spread the upper portion apart and fold down. Look at the illustrations to see the collapse in progress.

8

Repeat step 7 on the lower portion.

9

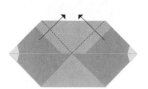

Fold the side flaps up to meet in the center.

10

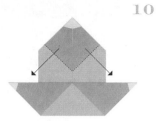

Fold the flaps out, using the pattern as a guide.

11

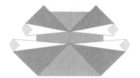

Spread apart the layers of the paws, and tuck in the tips. Look at the next illustration to see this in progress.

12

Flip over from side to side.

13

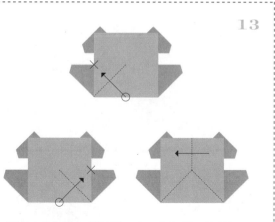

Bring circled point to "X", folding along dashed line. Unfold. Bring circled point to opposite side, again folding along dashed line. Unfold. Fold body in half. Triangular portion on bottom should collapse in as you fold.

14

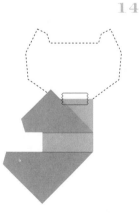

Attach koala head in between body with tape.

15

Final Result.

NEW CAL PALS CATWOMAN AND LOLA KITTY HIT THE TOWN

Lola Kitty

✳

origami paper on page: 131
number of sheets needed: 2

My name is Lola. I am in Hollywood right now pursuing an acting career. Last week, I was auditioning for a TV commercial and ran into Halle Berry. She called out encouragingly, "You go, girl!"

MAKE THE HEAD

| 1 | 2 | 3 | 4 |

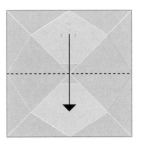

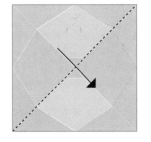

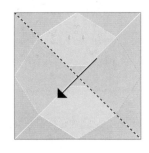

1 Flip over from top to bottom.

2 Fold in half. Unfold.

3 Fold top diagonally to meet right edge. Unfold.

4 Fold top diagonally to meet left edge. Unfold.

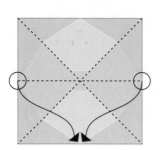

Pinch sides of paper where indicated with circles and carefully bring them in and down to meet the bottom edge, as shown by the arrows. Look at the next illustrations to see the collapse in progress.

5

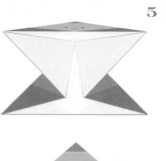

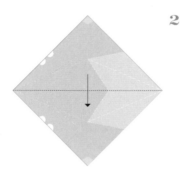

6

Fold sets of flaps on each side behind, using the pattern as a guide.

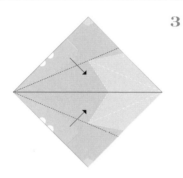

7

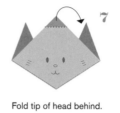

Fold tip of head behind.

8

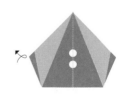

Final Result

MAKE THE BODY

1

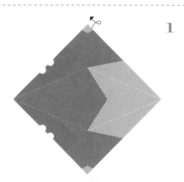

Flip over from top to bottom.

2

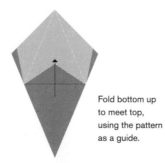

Fold in half. Unfold

3

Fold side edges to meet at center crease.

4

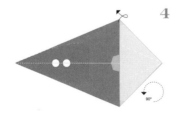

Flip model over and rotate 90 degrees counterclockwise.

5

Fold bottom up to meet top, using the pattern as a guide.

6

Flip over from side to side.

38

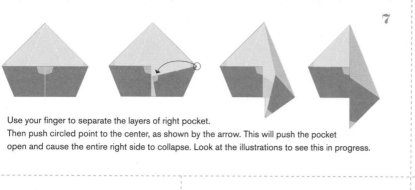

Use your finger to separate the layers of right pocket.
Then push circled point to the center, as shown by the arrow. This will push the pocket open and cause the entire right side to collapse. Look at the illustrations to see this in progress.

7

8

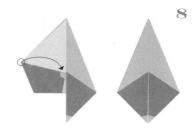

Repeat step 7 on the other side.

9

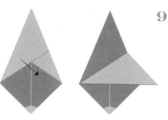

Fold top flap to right, using pattern as a guide. Unfold.

10

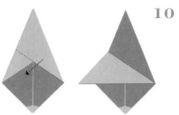

Fold top flap to left, using pattern as a guide. Unfold.

11

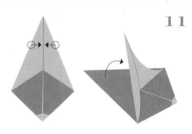

Pinch in the sides of the top flap until they meet in the center and then pull down. This will create a kitty tail that will pop out at you.

12

Flip over from side to side.

13

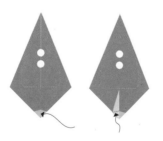

Open sides of left foot and tuck tip inside, using pattern as a guide.

14

Repeat step 13 on the right foot.

15

Fold kitty legs up, using the pattern as a guide. The legs should point straight up.

16

Flip over from side to side.

17

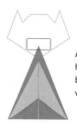

Attach kitty head to back of body with tape.

18

Final Result.

Wowo Puppy

*

origami paper on page: 133
number of sheets needed: 2

My name is Wowo. I am the most popular kid in school because whenever I wiggle my cute little tail, food magically appears. If you are nice, I'll share my food with you.

MAKE THE HEAD

1

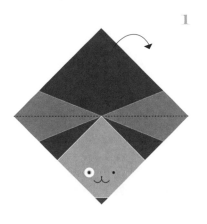

Fold in half.

2

Fold the sides in to meet at the center.

3

Fold the flaps up, using the pattern as a guide.

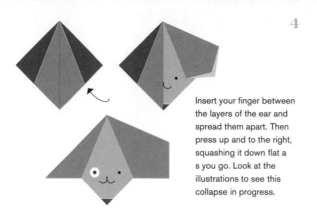

4

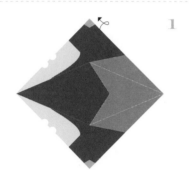

Insert your finger between the layers of the ear and spread them apart. Then press up and to the right, squashing it down flat a s you go. Look at the illustrations to see this collapse in progress.

5 Repeat step 4 on the other ear.

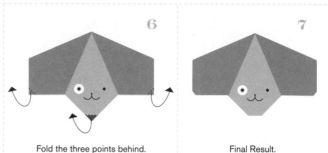

6

Fold the three points behind.

7

Final Result.

MAKE THE BODY

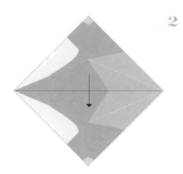

1

Flip over from top to bottom.

2

Fold in half. Unfold.

3

Fold side edges to meet at center crease.

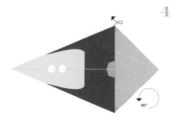

4

Flip over from top to bottom and rotate 90 degrees counterclockwise.

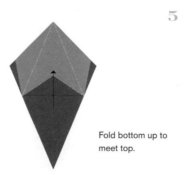

5

Fold bottom up to meet top.

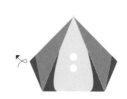

6

Flip over from side to side.

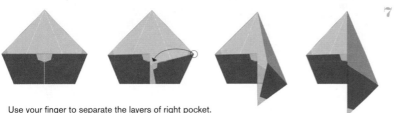

7

Use your finger to separate the layers of right pocket.
Then push circled point to the center, as shown by arrow. This will push the pocket open and cause the entire right side to collapse. Look at the illustrations to see this in progress.

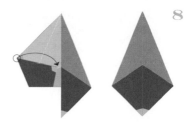

8

Repeat step 7 on other side.

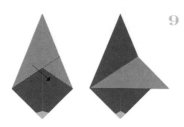

9

Fold top flap to right, using pattern as a guide. Unfold.

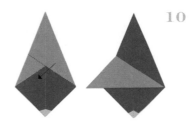

10

Fold top flap to left, using pattern as a guide. Unfold.

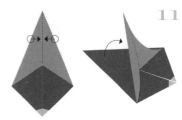

11

Pinch in the sides of the top flap until they meet in the center and then pull down. This will create a puppy tail that will pop out at you.

12

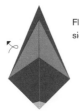

Flip over from side to side.

13

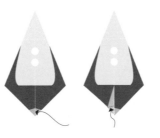

Open sides of left foot and tuck tip inside, using pattern as a guide.

14

Repeat step 13 on the right foot.

15

Fold puppy legs up, using the pattern as a guide.

16

Flip over from side to side.

17

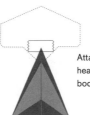

Attach puppy head to back of body with tape.

18

Final Result.

43

Weightless Laptop

✳

origami paper on pages: 135 & 137
number of sheets needed: 1

Just like a real laptop, this one conveniently stores a lot of memory. It has secret compartments where you can put movies tickets, photos, and other dainty trinkets for safekeeping.

1

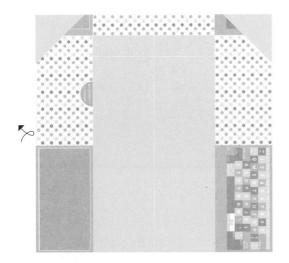

Flip over from side to side.

2

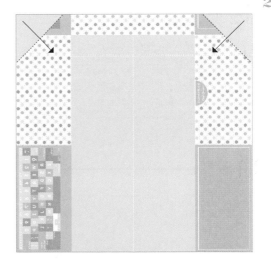

Fold the top corners in, using the pattern as a guide.

3

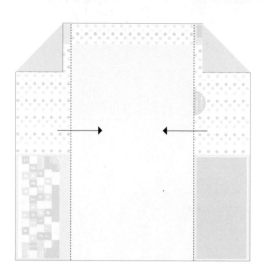

Fold the sides in, using the pattern as a guide.

4

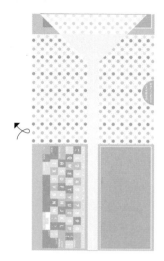

Flip over from side to side.

5

Fold the top edge down, to the white line.

6

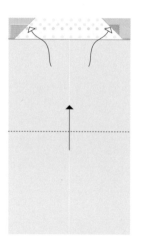

Fold the bottom edge up, using the pattern on the other side as a guide. Tuck the corners into the pockets.

7

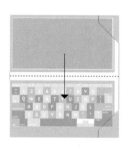

Fold your laptop in half to complete.

Final Result.

8

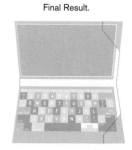

COMPUTER TERMS ALL GIRLS SHOULD KNOW

Bandwidth: How much data you can send through a network or modem connection.

Hardware: The machines, wiring, and other physical components of a computer.

IP address: A code made up of numbers separated by three dots that identifies a particular computer on the Internet.

Name server: Translates domain names into IP addresses. This makes it possible for a user to access a website by typing in the domain name instead of the website's actual IP address. For example, when you type in "www.girligami.com," the request gets sent to Girligami's name server, which returns the IP address of the Girligami website.

Software: The programs and other operating information used by a computer.

It's also good to know some common file extensions. Like these:

.doc Microsoft Word file.

.html Hypertext markup language page.

.jpeg or .jpg (Joint Photographic Expert Group) is the most common graphic file used on the Internet that almost every computer can open and read.

.mp3 (Moving Pictures Expert Group) is a common sound file.

.mpeg or .mpg (Moving Pictures Expert Group) is a common video file.

.pdf (Portable Document Format) is a file that allows you to view a document that was created in a different program, even if you don't have the program that it was originally created in.

.tiff or .tif (Tagged Image File Format) is a very common large, high-quality image file.

.txt A common file for text which many programs can open and read.

.xls Microsoft Excel file.

Computer term all girls should avoid:

Hacker: A clever or expert programmer who can gain unauthorized access to other computers.

THE ULTIMATE COOL NON-TALK SYSTEM

ORITALK

8 pm—
Leandro called
He can't wait
to see you
in Rome!

Ancient Phone

✳

origami paper on pages: 139–145
number of sheets needed: 2

Want to know what life was like before cell phones? Try dialing Italy, China, or Mexico on this phone.
You'll need a heck of an imagination, but you'll have all the minutes you want.

TO MAKE DIAL

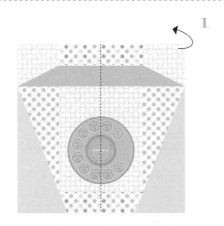

1

Fold in half behind.

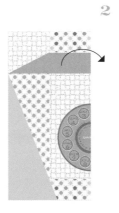

2

Unfold to reveal the white side.

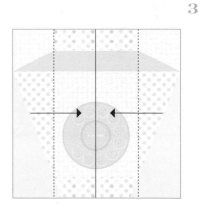

3

Fold the sides in to meet at the center crease. Unfold.

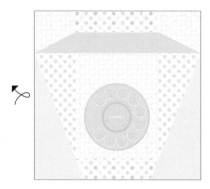

Flip over from side to side.

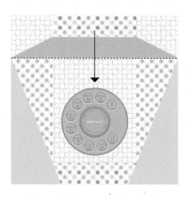

Fold the top edge down, using the pattern as a guide.

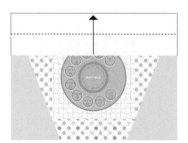

Fold the edge up to meet the top.

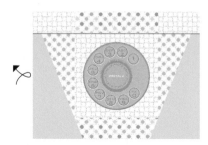

Flip over from side to side.

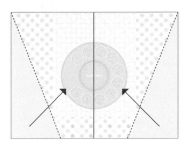

Fold diagonally so bottom corners meet at center crease.

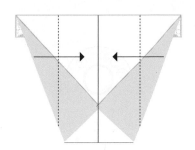

Fold sides in so top corners meet at the center crease.

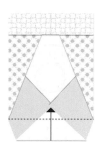

Fold the bottom edge up, using the pattern on the other side as a guide.

Unfold the sides halfway, so they are pointing straight up. Turn the model on its side.

Fold flap diagonally up, using the pattern on the other side as a guide. Unfold. Slip your finger into pocket, pinch the area indicated by the circle, and pull out to expand.

Flip over to other side of phone. Repeat step 12 with this side.

Cut along where dashed lines are marked. This is where your phone handle will go.

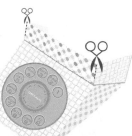

Final Result.

1

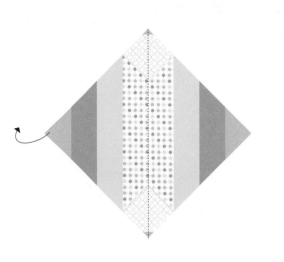

Fold in half. Unfold.

2

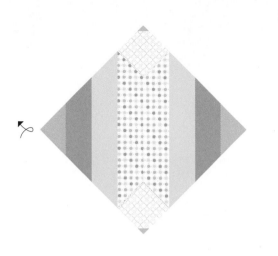

Flip over from side to side.

3

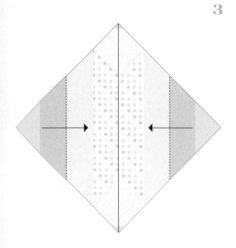

Fold sides in so tips meet at center crease.

4

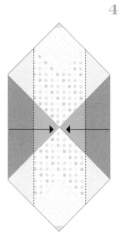

Fold sides in to meet at the center crease.

5

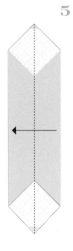

Fold in half.

6

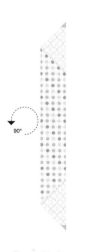

Rotate 90 degrees counterclockwise.

7

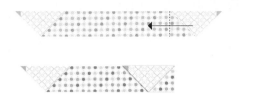

Fold right side in, using the pattern as a guide.

8

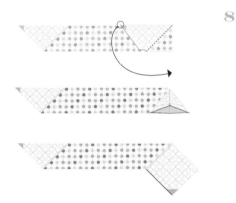

Slip your finger between the layers and bring the top flap down and to the right, squashing it as you go. Look at the illustrations to see the squash in progress.

9 Repeat steps 7-8 on the other side.

10

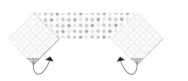

Fold the tips behind, using the pattern as a guide.

11

Attach the handle to the base, sliding one layer into the slots you cut.

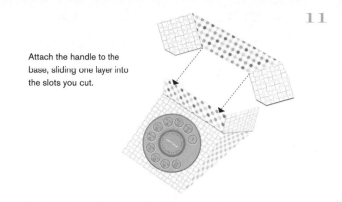

12

Final Result.

HOW TO SAY HELLO WHEREVER YOU ARE

* *hola* (Spanish)
* 你好 (*Ni Hao*) (Chinese)
* *Hallo* (Dutch)
* *Bonjour* (French)
* *Guten Tag* (German)—also means good day
* *Namasthe* (Hindi)
* *Konichiwa* (Japanese)
* *Salem* (Arabic)
* *Aloha* (Hawaiian)
* *Ciao*, or *buon giorno* (Italian)
* *YO! YO! YO!* (Brooklyn)

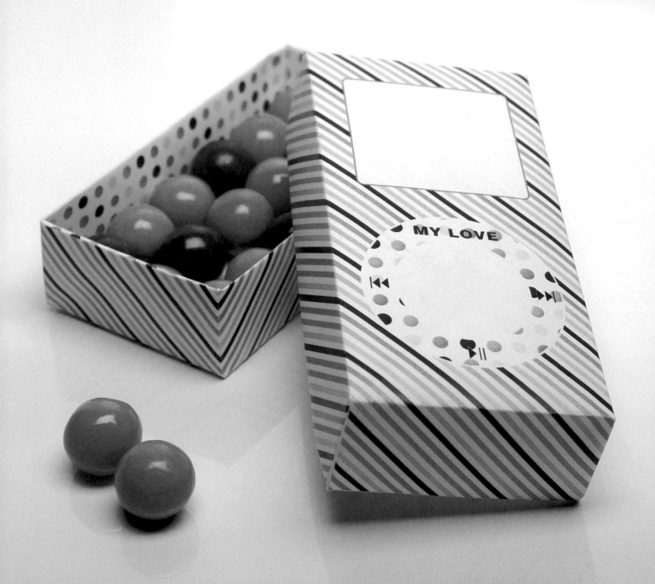

Zero-MB mp3 Player

✳

origami paper on pages: 147–153
number of sheets needed: 2

While your real iPod can hold your favorite music and videos, this awesome non-iPod
can store all your favorite small treasures.

MAKE THE TOP

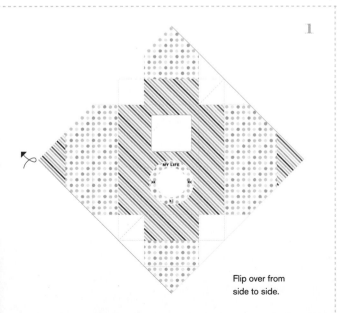

1

Flip over from
side to side.

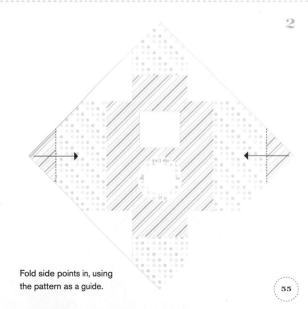

2

Fold side points in, using
the pattern as a guide.

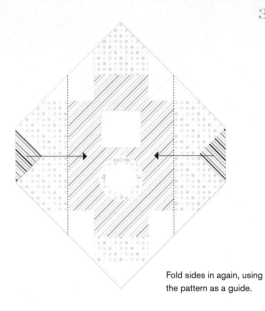

4

Fold sides in again, using the pattern as a guide.

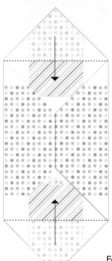

Fold in horizontally, using the pattern on the other side as a guide. Unfold.

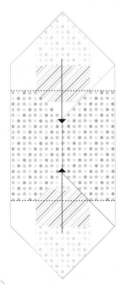

5

Fold in horizontally, using the pattern on the other side as a guide.

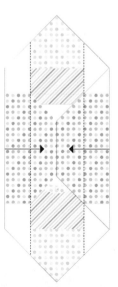

Fold in vertically to center.

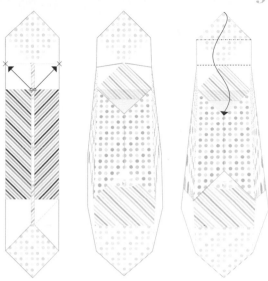

Fold each of the four sides diagonally along the dashed lines. Unfold.

Fold in horizontally at both the top and the bottom, using the pattern on the other side as a guide. Unfold.

Pinch the spots indicated by the circles and bring them up to the arrows. This will cause the sides to stand straight up. Then fold the top in and down to form the end of the box.

10   Repeat step 9 with the lower portion.

MAKE THE BOTTOM

11   Repeat steps 1–10 with bottom of iPod box.

12

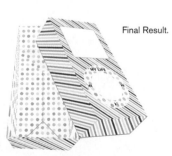

Final Result.

CUTE THINGS TO PUT INSIDE

* Items you use in daily life: barrettes, jewelry, lip gloss
* Items to give to someone you like (boys, girlfriends, Mom, Dad, sibling, grandparents)
* Items you love or want to collect: coins, movie stubs, stamps

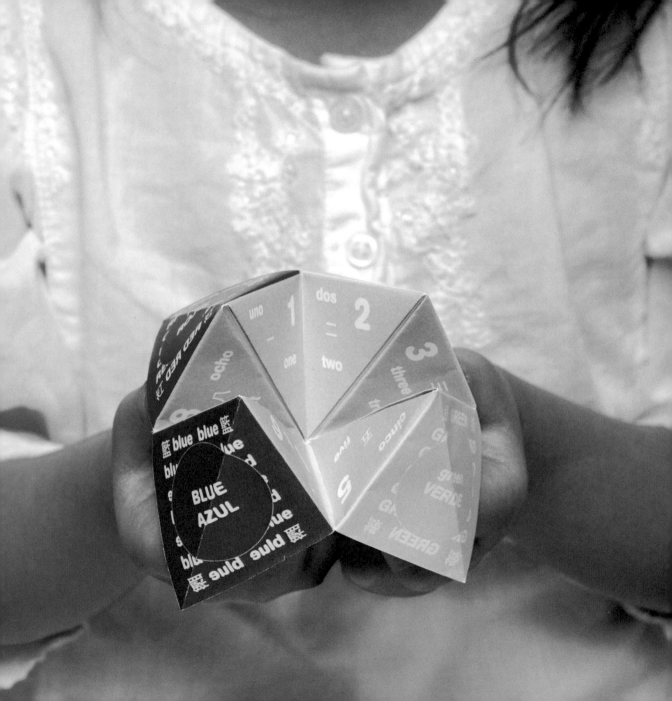

Fortune-Telling:

OLD FAVORITE, NEW TWIST

origami paper on pages: 155 & 157
number of sheets needed: 1

Roses are red, violets are blue; will this fortune be true for you?

1

Flip over from side to side.

2

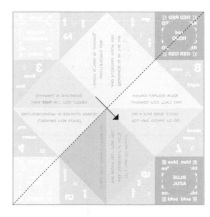

Fold top diagonally to meet right edge. Unfold.

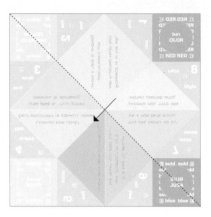

Fold top diagonally to meet left edge. Unfold.

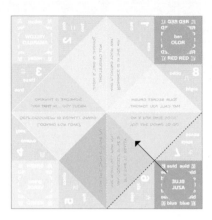

Fold one corner in to the center, using the pattern as a guide.

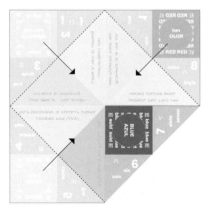

Fold the remaining three corners in to the center.

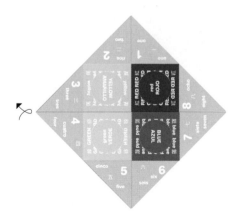

Flip over from side to side.

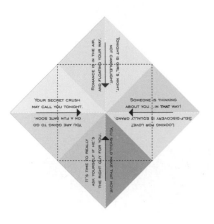

Fold the four corners in to the center.

Fold in half horizontally. Unfold.

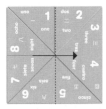

Fold in half vertically. Unfold.

Final Result.

HOW TO USE THE FORTUNE-TELLER

Number of players: 2 or 1 (but more fun with a friend)

1. Insert your index finger and thumb from both hands into the pockets and hold the fortune-teller so it is closed tight, with the colors facing up.
2. Have your friend choose one of the four colors. Spell that color out, while moving the fortune-teller in and out. When you get to the last letter, leave the fortune-teller open.
3. Now ask your friend to choose one of the numbers showing. Move the fortune-teller in and out that number of times. Leave it open at the last count.
4. Finally, have your friend choose one of the visible numbers. Open up that flap, and read the fortune.

Secret Love Note

✳

origami paper on pages: 159–163
number of sheets needed: 1

Roses are red, violets are blue, love notes make me swoon, and so do you.
Make someone blush and share a heartfelt note with someone you love!

1

Flip over from
top to bottom.

2

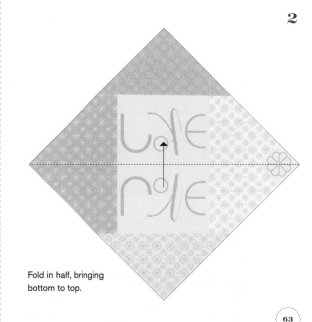

Fold in half, bringing
bottom to top.

3

Fold the left side in, using the pattern as a guide.

4

Fold the right side in, using the pattern as a guide.

5

Fold top flap to the right, using the white dashed line on the origami paper as a guide.

6

Fold the flap up on a diagonal, using the pattern as a guide. Unfold.

7

Slip your finger between the layers of the top flap. Pinch the point indicated by the circle and bring it up to the arrow, squashing as you go to form a diamond. The design will be revealed and should lie flat in center of model.

8

Fold horizontally downward. To close the love note, tuck top corner into the opening of the seal.

9

Final Result.

FLIPPED OUT

An "ambigram" is a graphic that spells out a word in its present form as well as in another direction or orientation.

TAKE NOTE! When this graphic of the word LOVE is flipped horizontally and then upside down, it spells NOTE. Cool, eh?

Yay! Presents

*

origami paper on pages: 165 & 167
number of sheets needed: 1

Roses are red, violets are blue, I love receiving presents, but I love to give too.
When this model is folded, it has a secret, hollow center where you can slip a cute mini-present.
Tie a ribbon around the model to close, then give it to someone you love.

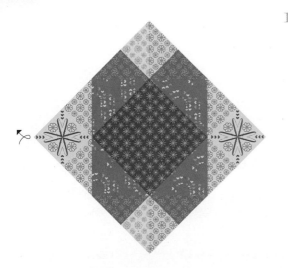

1

Flip over from side to side.

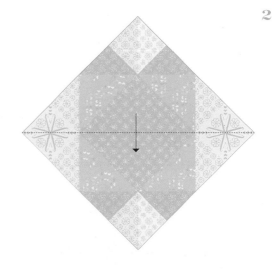

2

Fold in half horizontally. Unfold.

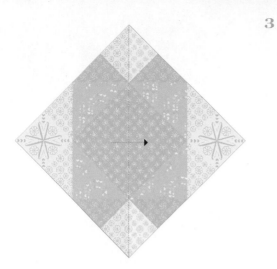

Fold in half vertically. Unfold.

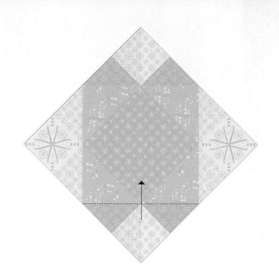

Fold the bottom corner up to the center.

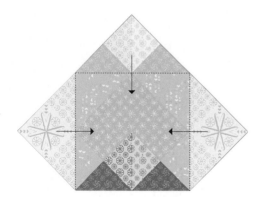

Fold the remaining corners in to the center.

Flip over from top to bottom.

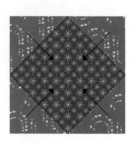

Fold the four corners in to
the center.

8

Flip over from side to side. Then rotate the paper 90 degrees clockwise.

9

Fold the model in half. Unfold.

10

Pull the flaps open and tuck them into each other until the sides meet. Look at the illustration to see this in progress.

11

Final Result.

12 After putting a present inside, you need to tie a ribbon around your model to close it.

IDEAS FOR THINGS TO PUT INSIDE YAY! PRESENTS

Handmade presents from *Girligami*:
    Vogue-It Earrings (page 99)
    Valentine Hearts (page 17) (add real Valentine candies to give your present an added surprise!)
    Critter Pins (page 103)

Other ideas you can wrap your love in:
    Chocolate kisses for your secret crush
    Sayings from fortune cookies for your best friend
    Jewelry for a friend's birthday
    Paper clips, rubber bands, and safety pins for the highly organized person in your life
    Band-Aid for a clumsy friend
    Stamps for a friend who loves correspondence
    Two quarters for a friend in case she needs to make an emergency call from a phone booth

A LOVE PATTERN

Did you notice? The letters in LOVE have been used to create the pattern in this origami paper.

  is composed of the letter L

  is composed of the letter O

  is composed of the letter V

  is composed of the letter E

In Hearts We Trust

✳

origami paper: large hearts on pages 169 & 171, and small hearts on pages 173 & 175
number of sheets needed: 1

Roses are red, violets are blue, fold this heart, and your dreams may come true.
You know that feeling when someone cares and wants the best for you and you feel the same way
about him or her? There is a word for that: love. Say it with an origami heart.

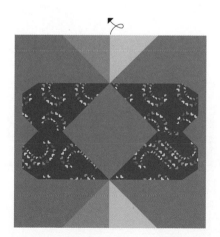

1

Flip over from top to bottom.

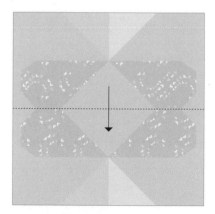

2

Fold in half. Unfold to reveal white side.

3

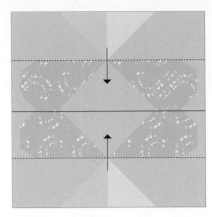

Fold the top and the bottom in to meet at the center crease.

4

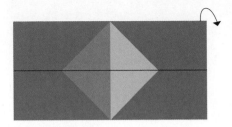

Fold the top half back along the existing crease.

5

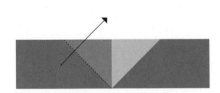

Fold the left side up, using the pattern as a guide.

6

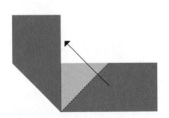

Repeat step 5 with the other side.

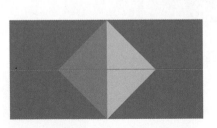

7

Bring the two flaps back down, and unfold along the center. This will return you to the same position as step 4.

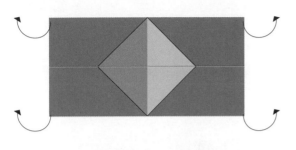

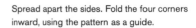

Spread apart the sides. Fold the four corners inward, using the pattern as a guide.

Reinforce the folds that lie along the center diamond shape. Then bring all four corners up to form the heart shape. This action will also cause the bottom diamond shape to invert, forming the base of the heart.

Fold the top four edges inward. Then place double-sided tape behind the two halves of the heart to hold them together.

Final result.

FIVE WAYS TO SHOW YOUR LOVE

* Call!
* Write!
* Smile!
* Do what you promised to do!
* Fold an origami heart!

Cocktail Dress

✻

origami paper on pages: 177 & 179
number of sheets needed: 1

Don't you wish you could pull a lovely dress like this one out of your closet to wear on your next date?
You'd be such a knockout!

1

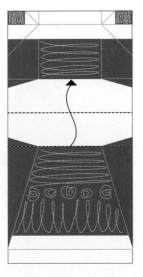

Form the waist by folding behind at the lower dashed line, and folding forward at the upper dashed line.

2

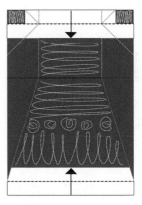

Fold the top and bottom in, using the pattern as a guide.

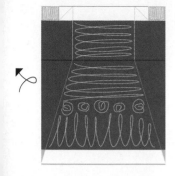

Flip over from side to side.

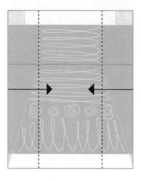

Fold the sides in so they meet at the center.

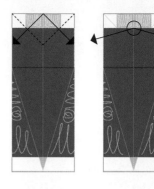

Fold the top corners out on a diagonal, using the pattern as a guide. Unfold. Then pinch the point indicated by the circle (top layer only) and pull it down and out to form the sleeves.

Fold the bottom right side out, using the pattern as a guide. Then flatten to form the A-line skirt of the dress. Repeat on the other side.

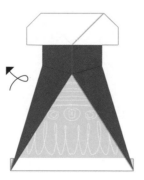

Flip over from side to side to reveal the dress. Finish by pulling the hem out so it is pointing straight out.

Final Result.

MAKE YOUR OWN HANGER

You'll need:

* 24-gauge wire
* Wire cutter
* Flat-nose pliers
* Round-nose pliers

1. Wrap wire around round-nose pliers to form the hook of the hanger.
2. Extend wire straight for about $^5/_8$ inch with the flat-nose pliers.
3. Bend wire diagonally to the right for about $^7/_8$ inch.
4. Bend wire to the left with flat-nose pliers for about 1 inch.
5. Bend wire diagonally to the right for about $^7/_8$ inch.
6. Wrap the remaining wire around the base of the hook of the hanger and snip off excess wire if necessary.

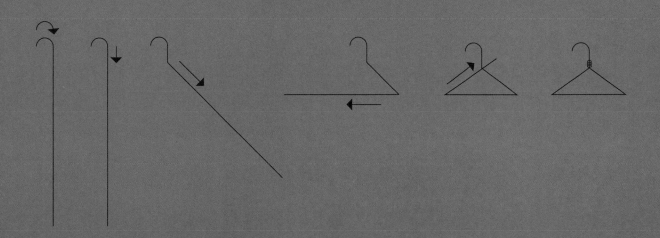

Trendy Tote

*

origami paper on pages: 181 & 183
number of sheets needed: 1

This dreamy tote would be perfect to sport on a girls' night out. Everyone would be so jealous!

1

2

Flip over from side to side.

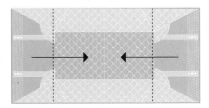

Fold the sides in, using the pattern on the other side as a guide. Unfold.

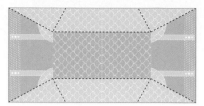

3

Fold as indicated, using the pattern on the other side as a guide. Unfold.

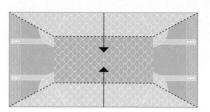

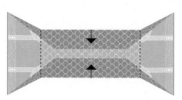

Fold each side of the middle portion in, so they meet in the middle.

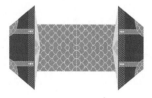

Fold the bottom of the bag in on both the left and right side.

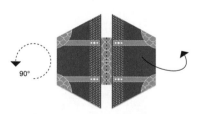

90°

Fold in half. Rotate the model 90 degrees.

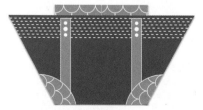

Final Result.

Use three small pieces of double-sided tape (or roll some regular tape together so that the ends meet) to adhere the middle part to each side of the bag.

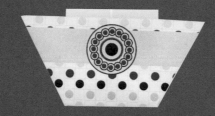

FASHION TIPS

Here are more ways to instantly
change your look:

* Add some jewelry.
* Wear cool tights.
* Slip into a pair of stiletto heels.
* Put your favorite shades on.
* Wrap your shoulders with a scarf.

Classy Ensemble

origami paper on pages: 185–191
number of sheets needed: 2

This lovely ensemble is perfect for a stroll in the park that just might lead to dinner at a café with that special someone. Don't you wish this outfit came in your size? A girl can dream…

TO MAKE PLEATED SKIRT

1

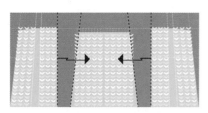

Fold as indicated, using the pattern as a guide. Then fold in to form pleats.

2

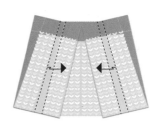

Fold as indicated again, using the pattern as a guide. Then fold in to form the second set of pleats.

3

Fold the side edges behind, using the pattern as a guide.

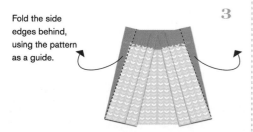

4

Fold the top edge behind, using the pattern as a guide.

5

Final Result.

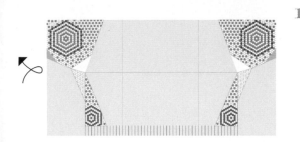

1

Flip over from side to side.

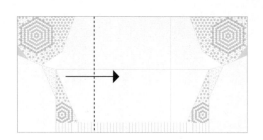

2

Fold the left side in, using the pattern on the other side as a guide. Unfold.

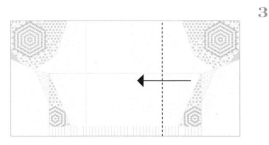

3

Repeat Step 2 with other side. Unfold.

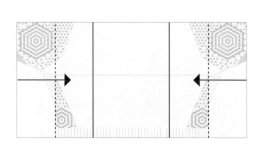

4

Fold both sides in to meet the creases.

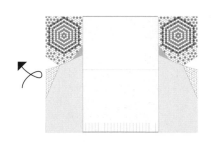

5

Flip over from side to side.

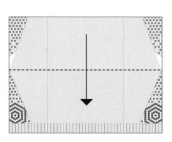

6

Fold down, using the line as a guide.

Flip over from side to side.

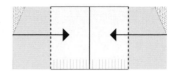

Fold the sides in to meet at the center.

To form the sleeves, pinch points indicated by circles and pull up and out. Then squash the sleeves down and fold on a diagonal, using the pattern as a guide.

Fold the points of the collar out, using the pattern as a guide.

Fold top tips of the sleeves behind, using the pattern as a guide.

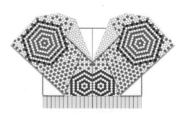

Final Result.

Foxy Pumps

✳

origami paper: large size on pages 193-204, and petite size on pages 205-207
number of sheets needed: 1

Now you can brag to all your girlfriends that you found a pair of stiletto heels that never hurt your feet.
They don't have to know these shoes are made from a pretty piece of paper—you can keep that part a secret.

<table>
<tr><td>1</td><td>2</td></tr>
</table>

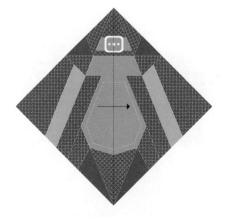

Fold in half. Unfold.

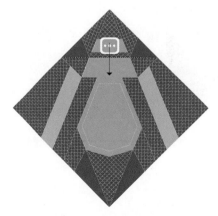

Fold the top point down, using the pattern as a guide. Unfold.

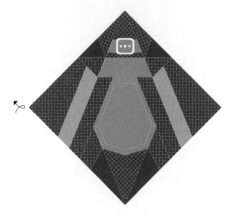

4

Flip over from side to side.

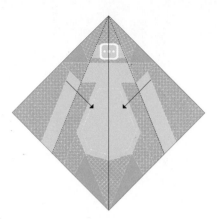

Fold the sides in, using the pattern as a guide. They should meet at the center crease.

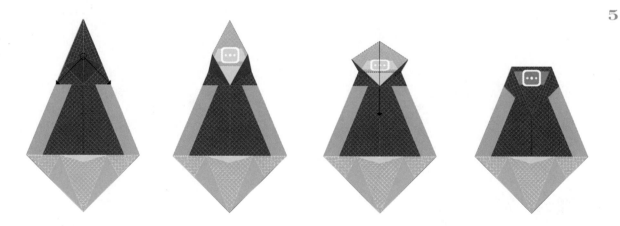

5

Stick your finger inside the pocket, and bring the point indicated by the circle down to the arrow on each side. This will cause the sides to open out. Then fold the top tip down, squashing it flat as you go.

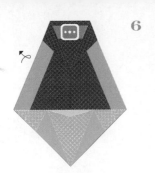

6

Flip over from side to side.

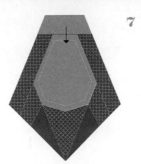

7

Fold top end down, using the pattern as a guide. Let toe of shoe pop out as you fold.

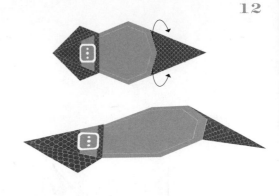

12

Form the heel by folding behind, using the pattern as a guide.

8

Flip over from side to side.

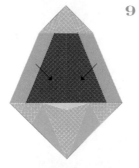

9

Fold the sides in, using the pattern as a guide.

13

Fold the shoe in half along the sole and the heel, and bring the heel down to complete.

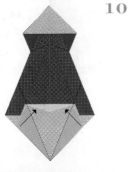

10

Fold the bottom edges in to meet at the center crease.

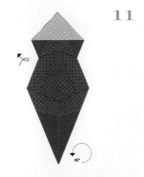

11

Flip over from side to side. Rotate 90 degrees counterclockwise.

Final Result.

14

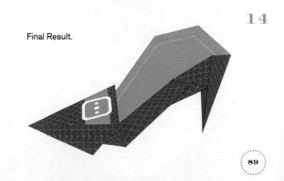

LET IT
BE

SMILE

WHAT TO MAKE

Turn your origami wonders into little gifts for yourself and your best gal pals. All craft supplies are easy to find in any crafts store, or online. For a list of specific resources, check out page 108, or log on to girligami.com for direct shopping links to purchase materials.

Love Is Everyday: Heart Ornaments

Create love ornaments to hang around your room or any space that needs extra TLC!
Here are two different variations.

VALENTINE HEARTS ORNAMENT

Materials you will need:
* 1/8-inch ribbon
* 2 1/8-inch glass ornaments from a crafts store
* double-sided tape
* scissors
* double-sided tape
* a completed Valentine Heart origami model (page 17)

Put it all together:
1. Cut a 6-inch length of ribbon.
2. Tape the Valentine Heart origami model to one end of the ribbon.
3. Thread the other end of ribbon through the glass ball hook.
4. Secure the ribbon by tying a knot. Trim off excess ribbon.

IN HEARTS WE TRUST ORNAMENT

Materials you will need:
* 1/8-inch ribbon
* double-sided tape
* scissors
* a completed In Hearts We Trust origami model (page 71)

Put it all together:
1. Cut an 8-inch length of ribbon.
2. Tape both ends of the ribbon into the center of the origami heart.

All-Occasion Greeting Cards

*

No need to spend a fortune in a card shop when you can make your own heartfelt greeting. Take plain card stock and grace it with stylish skirts, jackets, and pumps to make a greeting card that is great for birthdays or a simple hello.

Materials you will need:
* card stock or pre-cut blank cards
* double-sided tape
* any completed *Girligami* origami model

If you are cutting your card stock, you will also need:
* scissors
* craft knife
* metal ruler
* cutting mat

Optional:
* ribbon ($1/8$ or $3/8$ inch)
* extras like glitter glue, beads, feathers
* Magic Markers or glitter pens

Put it all together:
1. Cut card stock to size, if necessary.
2. Tape your origami model to the front of the card.
3. If you want to go further, add embellishments.
* Tape a ribbon on as an accent.
* Make a hanger (see page 77) and slip it into your origami shirt or dress.
* Accent with glitter glue or beads.

Fun It Up! Party Favor Bag

Dress up a casual party favor bag and fill it up with chocolates, lip gloss, a pocket mirror, or even *Girligami* projects—perfect for a swank birthday party.

Materials you will need:

* tiny paper bag (which can be purchased at any major crafts store)
* double-sided tape
* any completed Cute Critters origami model (pages 29–43) and/or any completed Valentine Heart origami model (page 17)

Put it all together:

1. Tape your origami model(s) onto the tiny bag.
2. Fill the bag with party favors, like chocolate, jewelry, makeup, and any other party-ish items you wish to include.

Vogue-It Earrings

❋

These are so vogue, you'll want to wear them right away! All jewelry-making materials
can be found at the jewelry-making section of any major crafts store.

HEART EARRINGS

Materials you'll need:

* safety pin
* pink beads
* shellac spray (or improvise with clear nail polish)
* stringing wire
* crimping pliers
* crimping tubes
* crimp bead cover
* 3-mm jump ring
* ear wires
* wire cutter
* flat-nose pliers
* a completed pair of mini In Hearts We Trust origami models (page 71)

Put it all together:

1. Use the safety pin to poke a tiny hole in the origami heart.
2. Thread stringing wire through the hole.
3. Thread 20 pink beads on each end of the wire.
4. Thread the ends of the stringing wire through the crimp tube and loop through the jump ring and back into the tube.
5. Pinch together the crimp tube with your crimping pliers.
6. Cover the crimp tube with crimp bead cover.
7. Thread your jump ring through a safety pin. Use the pin to hang up your origami model and then spray it with shellac (or paint with clear nail polish).
8. Let dry for 1-2 hours. Remove origami model from the safely pin.
9. Attach jump ring to an ear wire.

HIGH-HEEL EARRINGS

Materials you will need:

* safety pin
* shellac spray (or improvise with clear nail polish)
* eye pins
* ear wires
* wire cutter
* flat-nose pliers
* round-nose pliers
* a completed pair of mini Foxy Pumps origami models (page 87)

Put it all together:

1. Use the safety pin to poke a tiny hole through the top of the heel.
2. Thread an eye pin through the hole.
3. Use the round-nose pliers to make a loop with the eye pin.
4. Holding the loop you just made with the flat-nose pliers, wrap the remaining eye pin around 3-4 times.
5. Use wire cutters to trim any excess eye pin.
6. Thread the loop you made in steps 3-4 through a safety pin. Use the pin to hang up your origami model and then spray it with shellac (or paint with clear nail polish).
7. Let dry for 1-2 hours. Remove origami model from the safely pin.
8. Hook an ear wire onto each.

Smashing Fun Necklaces

*

The abstract and geometric features of origami make for great necklaces.

Materials you'll need:
* silver ball chain, 16 inches long
* 5-mm jump ring
* safety pin
* eye pin
* flat-nose pliers
* any small, flat, *Girligami* origami model. Some good ones to choose from are the Cool Cupcake, Sweet and Swirly Ice Cream, Lacy Jacket, Pleated Skirt, and Trendy Tote

Put it all together:
1. Use the safety pin to poke a tiny hole through the midpoint at the top of the model.
2. Using flat-nose pliers, open the jump ring and thread it through the hole.
3. Use flat-nose pliers to close the jump ring.
4. Thread silver ball chain through jump ring.

Critter Pins

Express your love for cute critters by pinning one on your jacket, bag,
or even your bulletin board.

Materials you will need:
* 1-inch pin back with self-adhesive backing (available at any major crafts store)
* any Cute Critter origami model (you'll only need the head)

Put it all together:
1. Remove backing from pin back.
2. Stick pin onto the back of cute critter head.

Colorific Magnets

These pretty magnets will transform any plain metal object around you into a colorific space.

Materials you will need:
* magnetic strip with self-adhesive backing (available at any craft or office supply stores)
* scissors
* any completed origami model from the Sweets and Treats chapter (pages 17–27)

Put it all together:
1. Cut magnetic strip to fit your origami model.
2. Peel the backing off the magnetic strip and stick to the back of your origami.

Hanging Notepads

Need to multitask? Shopping, list-making, reading, all the 100 things you need and want to do.
Get them done (in style) with these pretty list-making, write-down-whatever's-on-your-mind notepad.
They also do double-duty as bookmarks, so you can note your favorite passages while you're reading,
mark down things you want to buy, and record all the intimate thoughts from your beautiful mind.

Materials you will need:
* precut tags (3¹/₄-inch x 5¹/₄-inches is a good size)
* little pad of self-adhesive notes (like Post-Its™)
* self-adhesive page markers
* embellishments, such as tiny dried flowers
* double-sided tape
* hole punch
* ¹/₈-inch ribbon
* any completed *Girligami* origami model

Put it all together:
1. Use double-sided tape to stick your origami onto the tag.
2. Tape the self-adhesive notepad below the origami.
3. Tape on any embellishments.
3. Punch a hole in the top of the tag, and tie a piece of ribbon through it for hanging.

Top Picks:

MY FAVORITE RESOURCES

Here are some of my favorite origami and paper crafting resources, starting with my own business:

Finger Magic: Origami Designed to Be Better

Origami jewelry, kits, parties, and books

Join the mailing list for new product releases, pretty postcards via snail mail, and cool codes via e-mail.

www.fingermagic.com

Hanko Designs

Asian rubber stamps, Japanese origami, and Washi papers

www.hankodesigns.com

Paper Animations

Paper models you make that move

www.paperanimations.com

Origami Blog

A blog dedicated to the joys of origami and covering everything from concepts to products to inspiration.

www.origamiblog.com

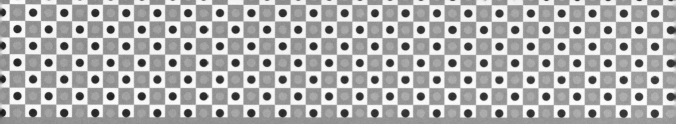

Here's where I would skip to and purchase my jewelry-making supplies.

Michael's Arts and Craft   www.michaels.com
Joann   www.joann.com
Hobby Lobby   www.hobbylobby.com

- -

Here's where I would hop to and purchase my card stock for all my card-making endeavors.

Dick Blick Art Materials   www.dickblick.com
Pearl Art & Craft Supply   www.pearlpaint.com
Paper Source   www.paper-source.com

- -

Here are my favorite San Francisco independent crafty & art shops.

Arch
99 Missouri, San Francisco, CA 94107
www.archsupplies.com

University Art
128 Spear Street, San Francisco, CA 94105
www.universityart.com

Paper Tree
1743 Buchanan Mall, San Francisco CA 94115
www.paper-tree.com

Flax Art & Design
1699 Market Street, San Francisco, CA 94103
www.flaxart.com

THE PAPERS

LET'S KISS

ALL MINE

LET IT BE

WHATEVER

ALL MINE

COOL

WHATEVER

SMILE

VALENTINE
HEARTS
(project on page 17)

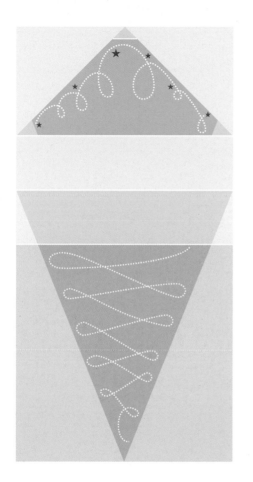

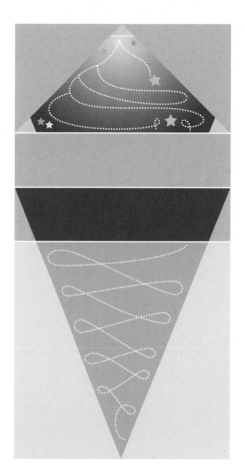

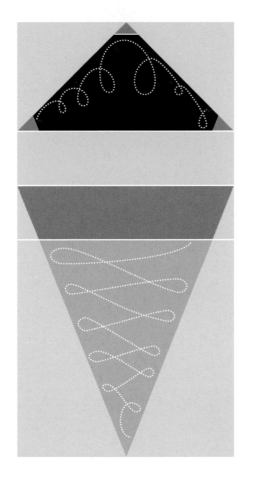
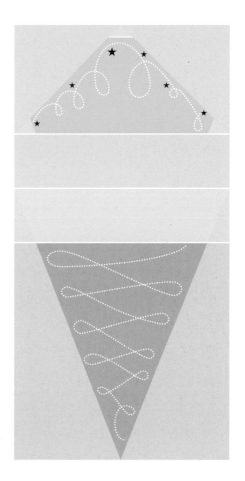

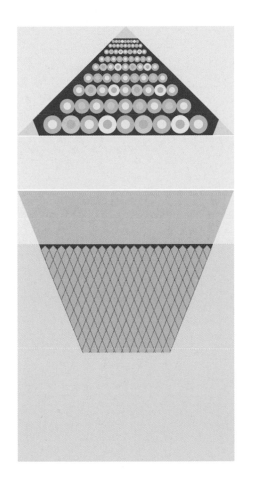
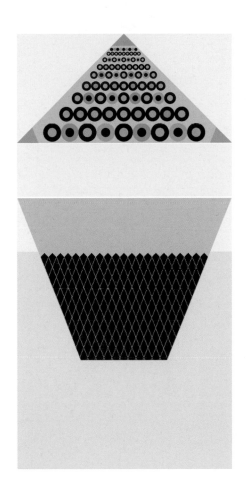

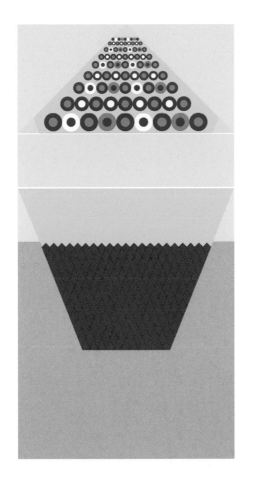
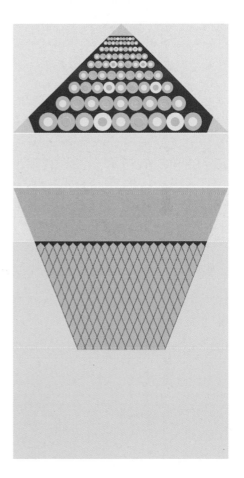

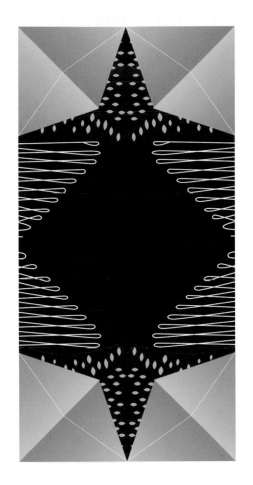 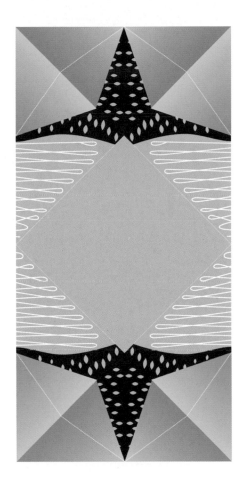

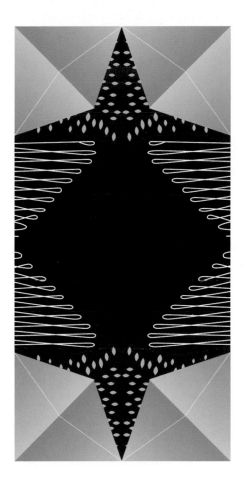

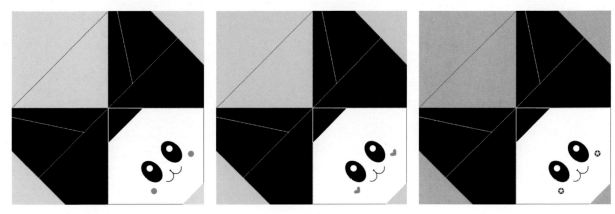

HEAD

(EXTRA HEAD FOR CRITTER PIN PROJECT ON PAGE 103)

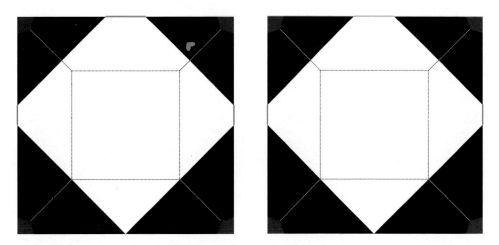

BODY

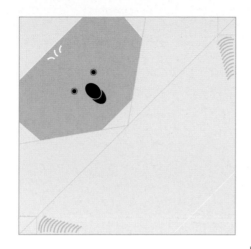
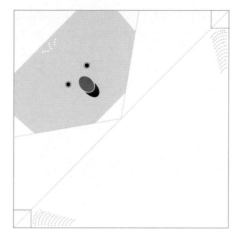

HEAD

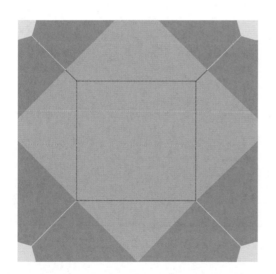

BODY

COCA KOALA (project on page 33)

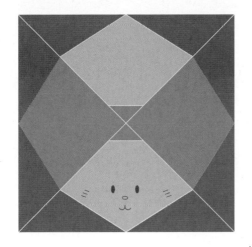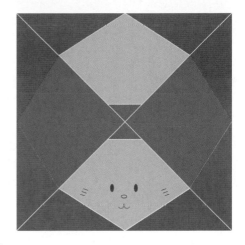

HEAD

BODY

LOLA KITTY (project on page 37)

HEAD
(EXTRA HEAD FOR CRITTER PIN PROJECT ON PAGE 103)

BODY

WOWO PUPPY (project on page 41)

WEIGHTLESS LAPTOP
(project on page 45)

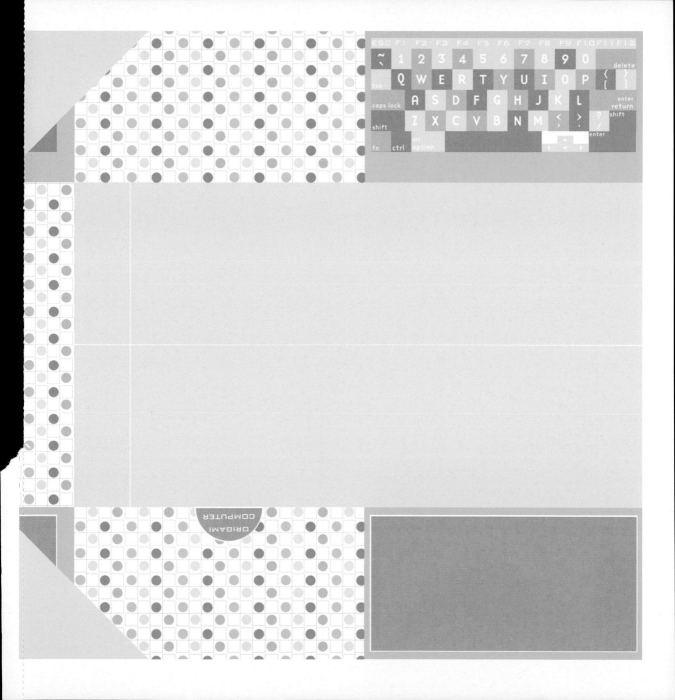

ORIGAMI COMPUTER

WEIGHTLESS LAPTOP
(project on page 45)

HANDLE OF PHONE (PATTERN A)

HANDLE OF PHONE (PATTERN B)

ANCIENT PHONE   (project on page 49)

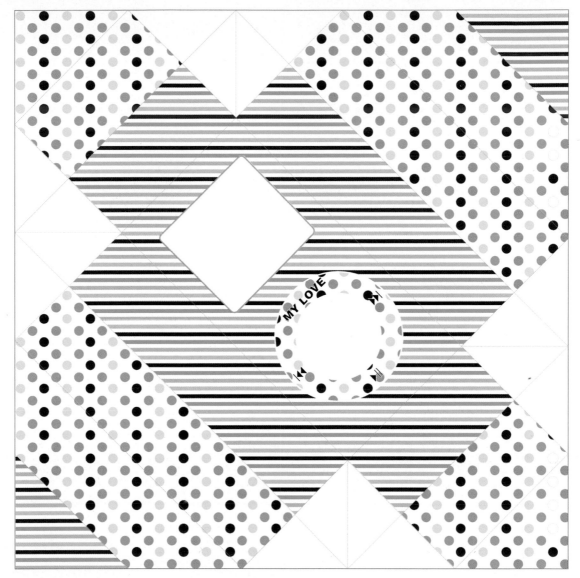

TOP (PATTERN B)

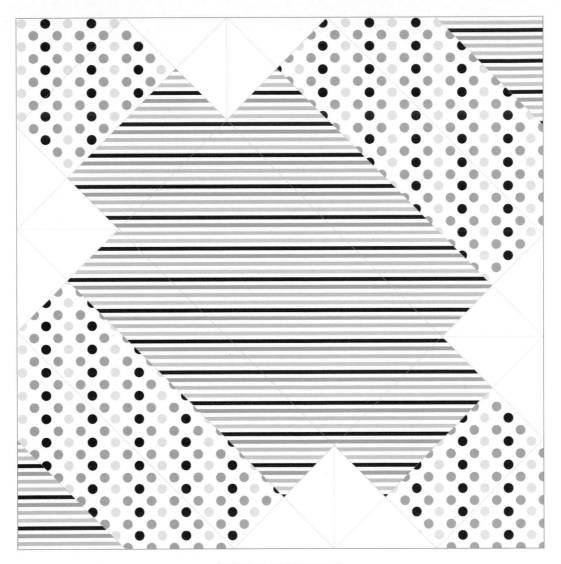

BOTTOM (PATTERN B)

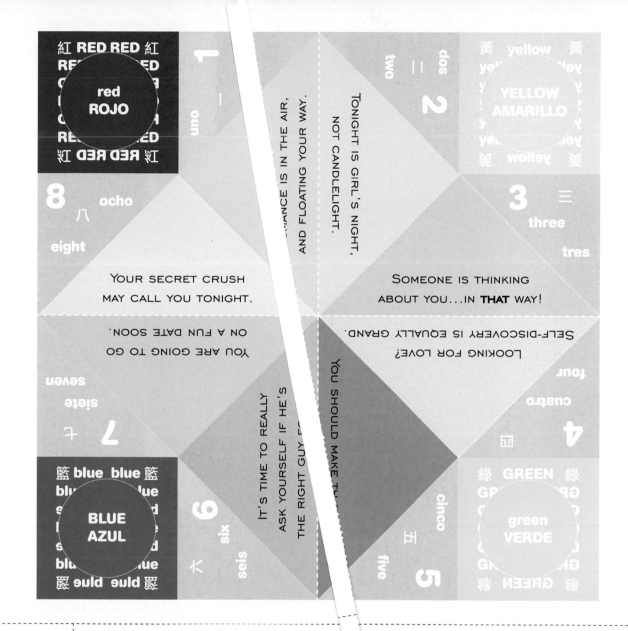

SECRET LOVE NOTE   (project on page 63)

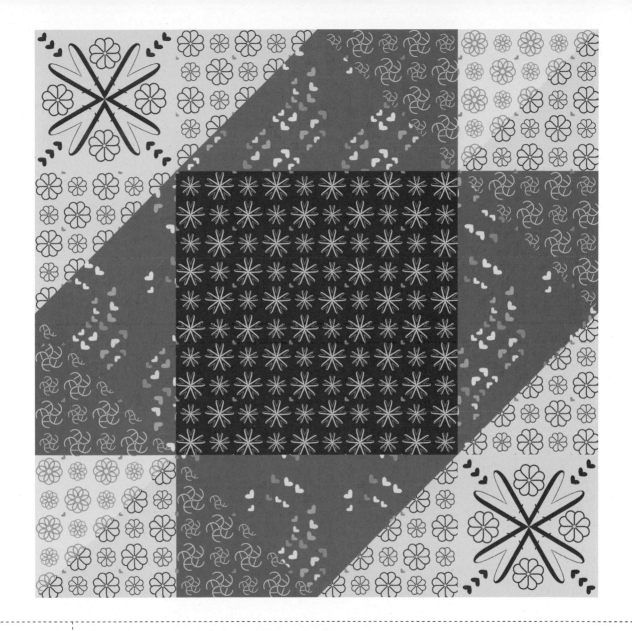

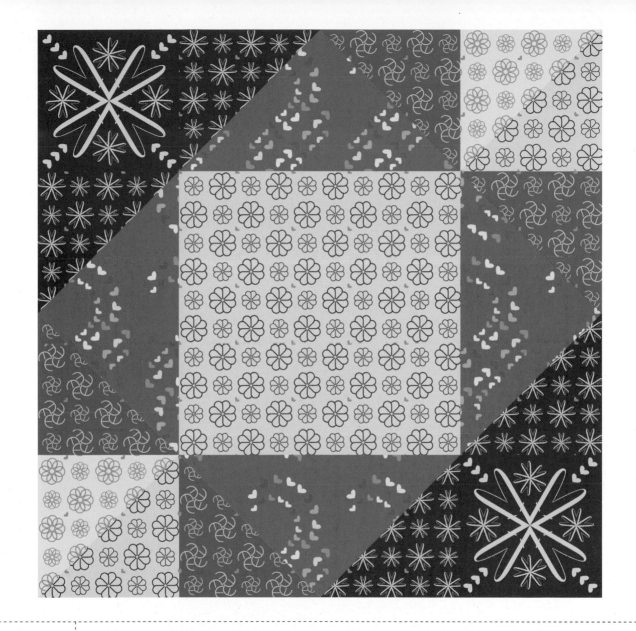

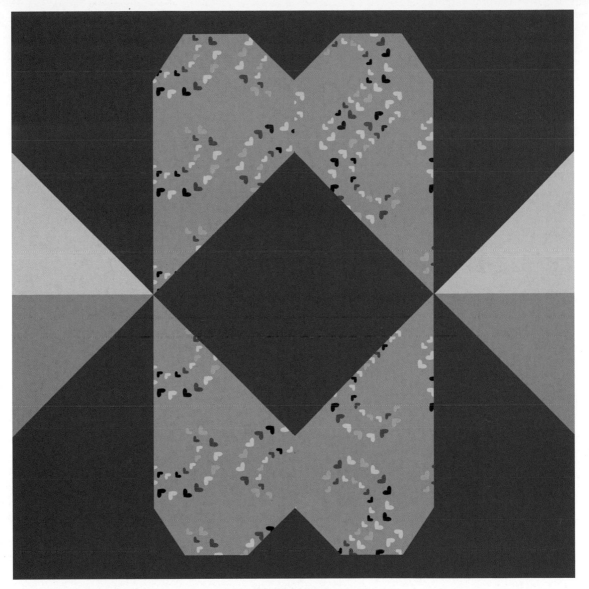

LARGE SIZE

IN HEARTS WE TRUST   (project on page 71)

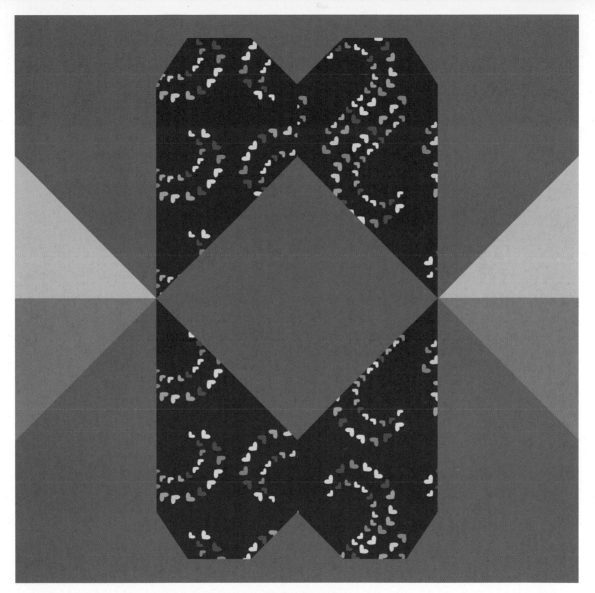

LARGE SIZE

PETITE SIZE

IN HEARTS
WE TRUST
(project on page 71)

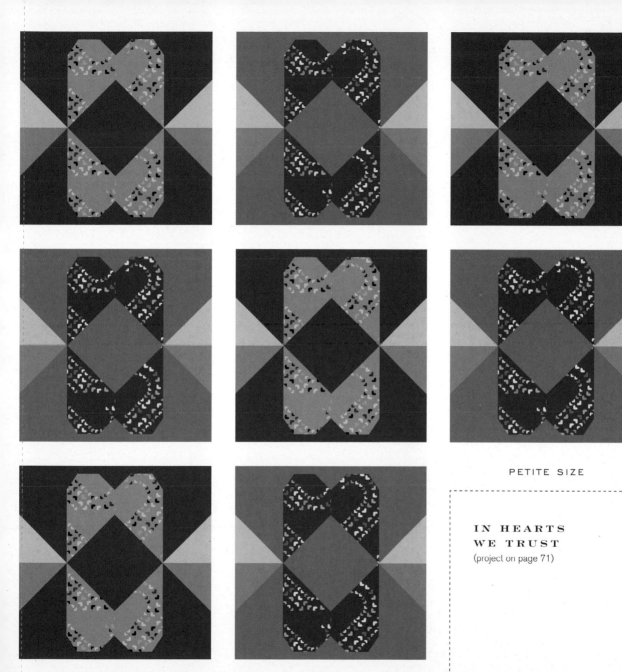

PETITE SIZE

IN HEARTS
WE TRUST
(project on page 71)

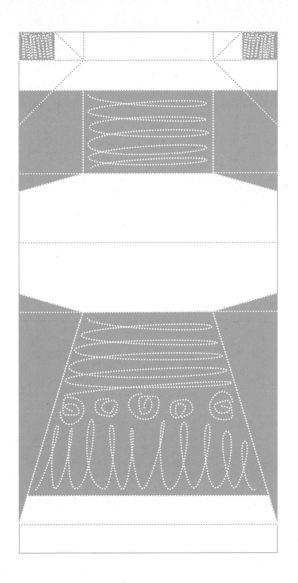
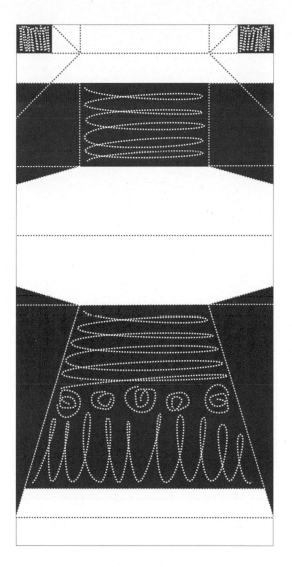

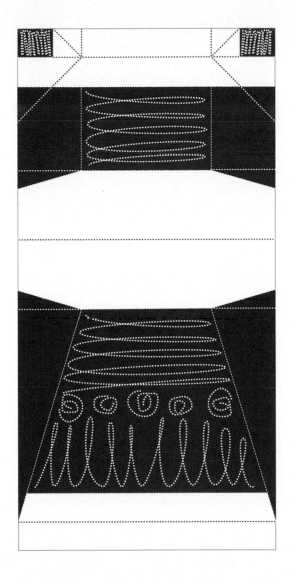
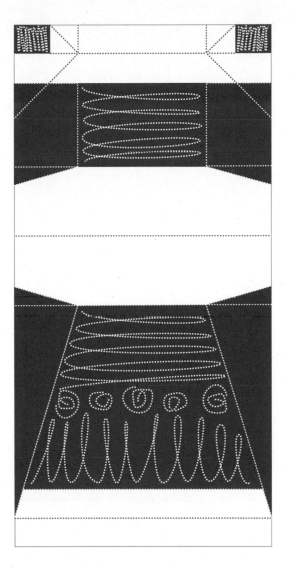

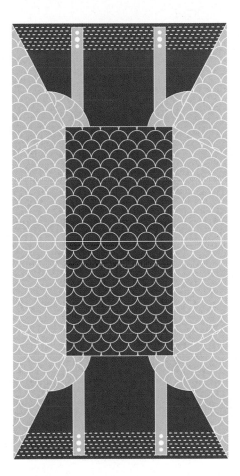

TRENDY TOTE   (project on page 79)

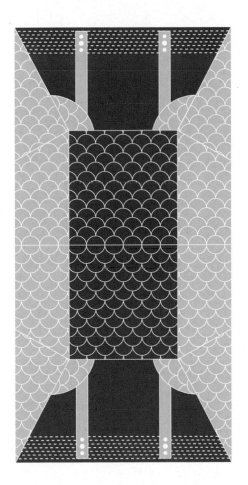
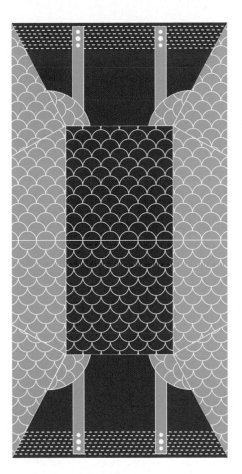

TRENDY TOTE (project on page 79)

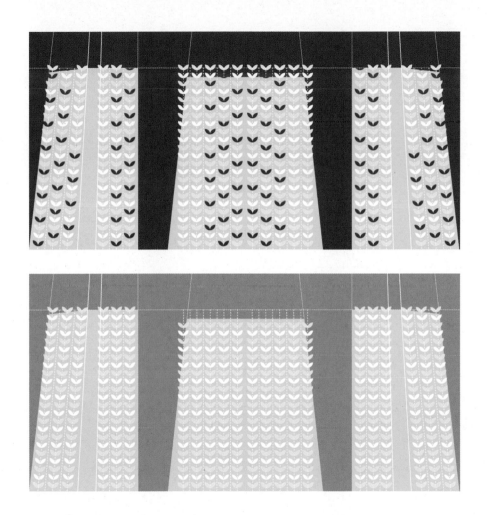

PLEATED SKIRT (project on page 83)

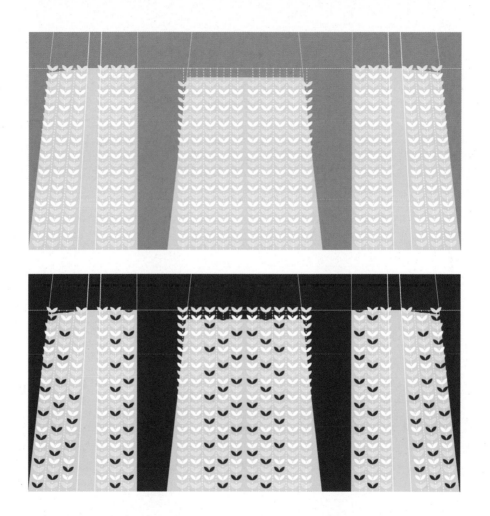

PLEATED SKIRT (project on page 83)

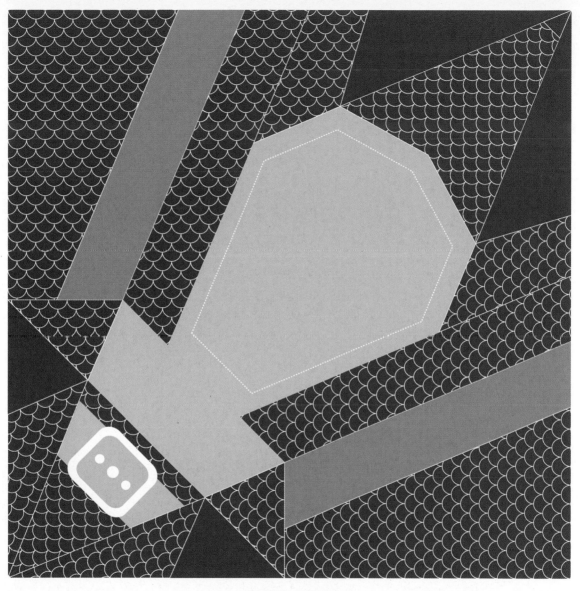

LARGE SIZE

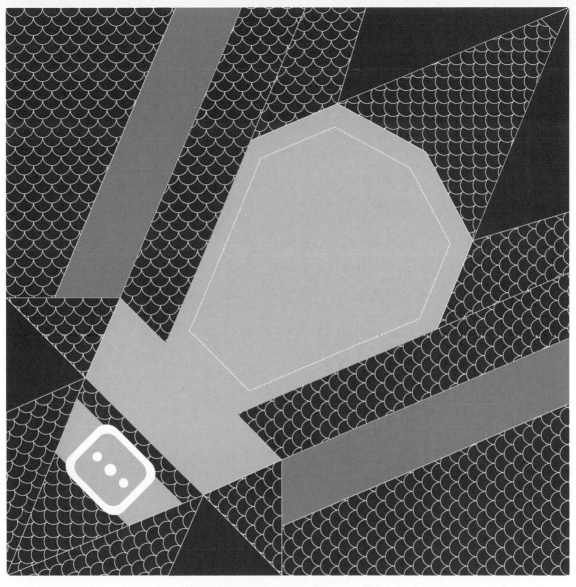

LARGE SIZE

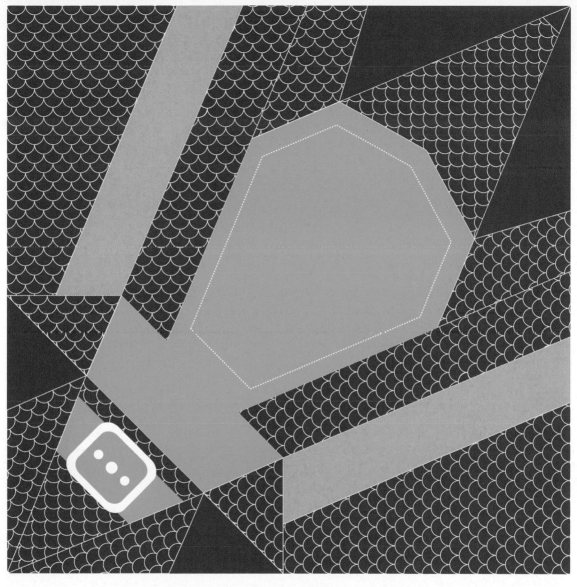

LARGE SIZE

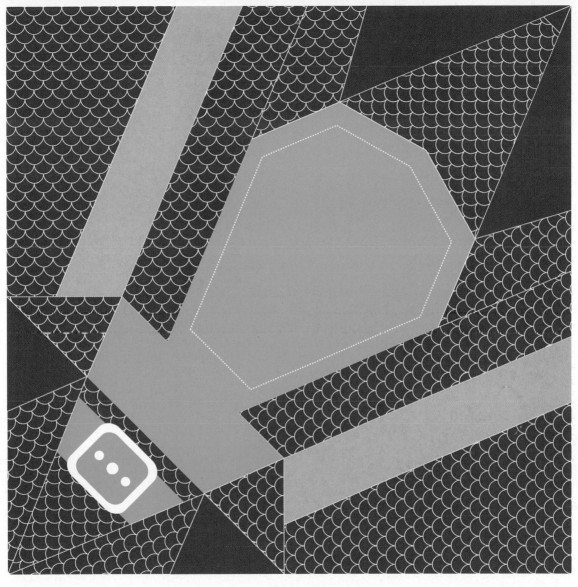

LARGE SIZE

FOXY PUMPS (project on page 87)

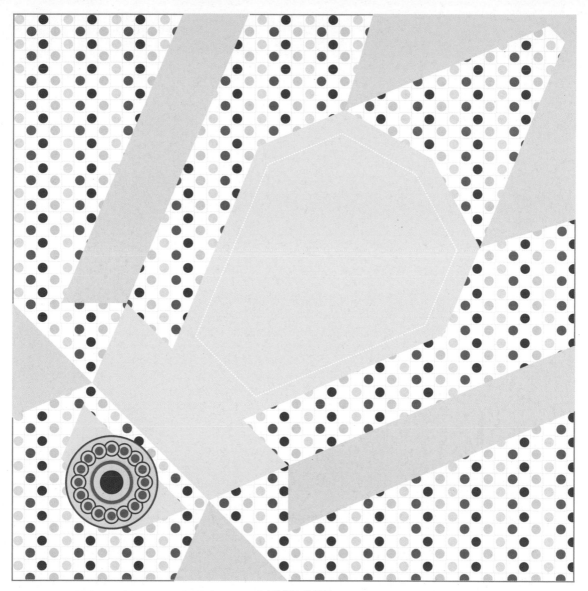

LARGE SIZE

FOXY PUMPS   (project on page 87)

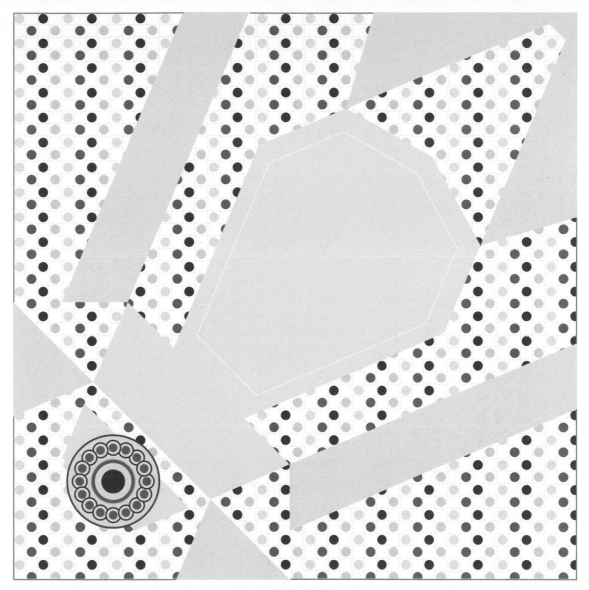

LARGE SIZE